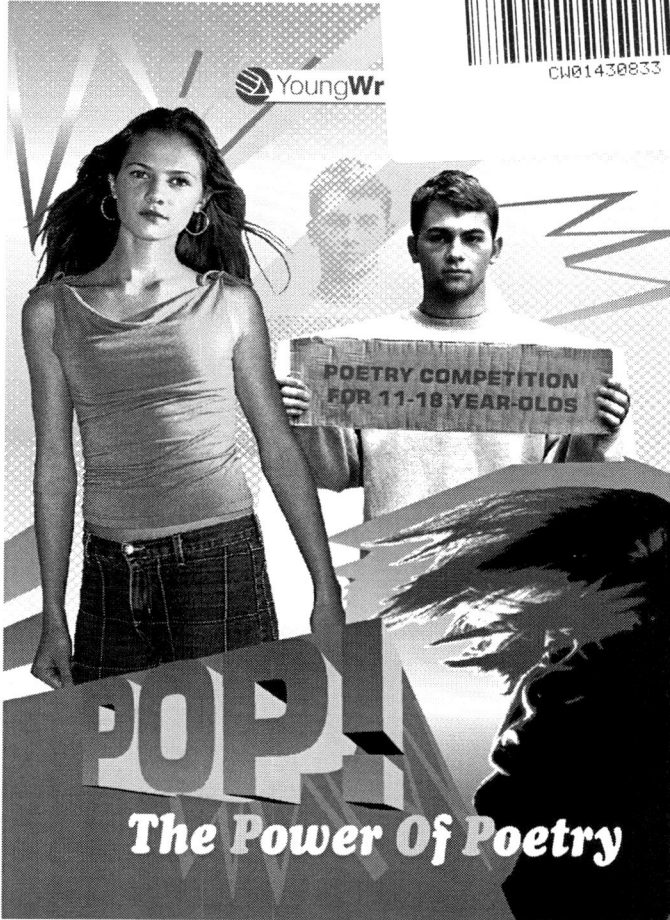

YoungWr

POETRY COMPETITION
FOR 11-18 YEAR-OLDS

POP!

The Power Of Poetry

International Inspirations

Edited by Claire Tupholme

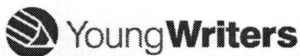

Young**Writers**
First published in Great Britain in 2006 by:
Young Writers
Remus House
Coltsfoot Drive
Peterborough
PE2 9JX
Telephone: 01733 890066
Website: www.youngwriters.co.uk

SB ISBN 1 84602 407 2

Foreword

This year, the Young Writers' *POP! - The Power Of Poetry* competition proudly presents a showcase of the best poetic talent selected from thousands of up-and-coming writers nationwide.

Young Writers was established in 1991 to promote the reading and writing of poetry within schools and to the young of today. Our books nurture and inspire confidence in the ability of young writers and provide a snapshot of poems written in schools and at home by budding poets of the future.

The thought, effort, imagination and hard work put into each poem impressed us all and the task of selecting poems was a difficult but nevertheless enjoyable experience.

We hope you are as pleased as we are with the final selection and that you and your family continue to be entertained with *POP! International Inspirations* for many years to come.

Contents

International School Ibadan, Nigeria

The English International College, Spain

The Poems

Indigenous Spectre

As cold and beaten legs walked on past me,
The frozen and tank imprinted streets of the city looked at me
with unrevealing eyes.
The chill of the night seemed to bind the sad and tired shoulders
of those who bore them.
Long, droopy eyes of the figures that were foreign to this place,
Hardly lifted them up to glance at me as I advanced towards
my unknown terminus.
Unaware that the evil passionless, dead but alive cold,
held me prisoner to its uneasy spirit.
I thought that I might decease into the night,
That I'd become the very enemy that was like a swindler,
Taking what isn't theirs to become, only vaster.
Having no particular reason in doing so,
The dead figurines and I didn't even try to discord it,
Too afraid to attempt anything,
For it was too powerful.
So we trudged on in complete surrender to this unseen assailant,
Dead, but alive at the same time.

Gjoshua Gibbons (15)
Bermuda Institute, Bermuda

Let Your Hair Down

In the world that we live in today
People worry too much about what others might say,
You're afraid to show people who you are inside.
So you act as if you're happy but it's sadness you hide,
How would people know who you really are,
If you just glow like the moon.
Instead of shining like a star?
You put on a mask because you're afraid of what
people might think
But if you don't show your talents, your talents would shrink.
So express yourself and no longer frown
And do me a favour and let your hair down.

Sharla Mercado (12)
Bermuda Institute, Bermuda

I Wish . . .

I wish that we were all one race
So we wouldn't be in such a hurry
To kill each other's ace

I wish countries could get along
So we can sing one worldwide anthem song

I wish there were no killings or illnesses
Just peace, joy, love and happiness

I wish no kids would think of bad thoughts
Like blowing up buses or any of that sort

I wish there were no bombs, guns or anything that creates pain
I mean, what will we all gain?
Nothing, that's what, but days of rain

Nothing until we all learn to get along
And sing one big, happy peace song

I wish . . . I wish that this would all come true
But it won't, I think this is the world's biggest blues.

Demetria Packwood (12)
Bermuda Institute, Bermuda

The Sky

The sun, the moon, the stars,
All admire who you are.
Things are near,
Things are far.

All I want is them to stay,
Please I beg you, don't go away,
There they are and there they go,
I will always see them tomorrow.

Angelina Todd (11)
Bermuda Institute, Bermuda

The Sky

The moonlit sky is such a beautiful sight,
But what a shame you only see it at night,
The stars are dazzling with all their might,
The sun is very bright with its atmospheric flares,
But who cares,
Who spends all night and stares?
I wish I could see the sun and the moon,
So often I could chat to them all afternoon.
But my dream will never come true,
If it did I would share it with you!

Maysoon Mehdi (11)
Dhahran British Grammar School, Saudi Arabia

Space

I always wonder what's in space,
Maybe there's a galactic race.
I can only see the stars,
Like the headlights on cars.
But aliens might leave behind a trace.

Every night I build up my rocket,
I keep a smaller version in my pocket.
I attach big things,
For example huge wings.
And I'll never leave without my chocolate.

All the kids think it's cool
But there's a problem,
There's no fuel!

Nathan Killen (11)
Dhahran British Grammar School, Saudi Arabia

My Class

I don't think anyone would like to be in my class.
The noise is deafening, everyone goes mad.
The headmaster is sick of seeing us, day after day,
I think it all started some time in May . . .

Bobby spilt the paint all over Jenny's clothes,
Kelly got annoyed and ran on home!
Benny put clay all over Sally's hair,
Jessica broke her leg trying to fly in mid-air!

Barry kicked the teacher,
Boy, was Miss Brown mad!
Sue had a fight with Mary,
Little Mickey was extremely sad.

So now you know what my class is like.
Very, very weird!
I hope you feel sorry for me
As I'm the only normal one there!

Caroline Fitzgerald (12)
Dhahran British Grammar School, Saudi Arabia

Time

Time is a strange thing
You can't hold it or touch it, or see it, but you know it's there.
That peaceful nothingness that you know is something,
If you could see time, I wonder what it would look like,
Maybe it's a good thing we can't see time
It makes it more mysterious.
Some people say they can stop time, or go back in time,
I think time should just be left alone.
We have come to rely on time for a lot of things,
We buy watches and clocks
But still no one really knows what time is.
No one really understands it.
It can make us older, wiser, stronger
Maybe it shouldn't be understood.
Oh, it's 6 o'clock,
Time for supper.

Freya Carberry (11)
Dhahran British Grammar School, Saudi Arabia

Poems

Poems are great to express what you're feeling,
Say if you were down in the dumps or as high as the ceiling.
They can be about lions, chickens or even a plane,
Or about a horse's silky soft mane.
You can talk about the darkness of the night
Or the bright shine of day.
You can talk about people and what they say,
You could express the way you feel about pictures,
Or if you like wearing flowery huge knickers!
You could grab people's attention by having big
Exciting words,
Or you could just shout about it and fly as high as a bird.
The greatest poems were about lots of different things,
Like the park in the snow or the monkey and how he swings.
I like poems and the way that they are,
'Cause if you're a poet, you will go very far!

Freya Cooper (11)
Dhahran British Grammar School, Saudi Arabia

Waves

Waves, swirling, thrashing around me,
Sweeping me off my feet,
Some are soft, they move without a sound,
Others are as hard as rock, roaring on the sand.

No one can really tell the colour of the sea,
Near the shore, it's calm, blue and green
And in the deep, blue as dark as black.

The mysteries of the ocean and waves,
Have never been foretold.
There are many tales that no one knows,
And they never will.

Catherine Brandt (11)
Dhahran British Grammar School, Saudi Arabia

Aliens Are Invading!

Eating my breakfast,
Spreading on butter.
A knock at the door
I start to stutter.
'Who's there? Who's there?'
I run from the table, no time to spare!
I look through the peephole to see what I can see,
There's a little alien pointing a ray gun at me!

'Come with I,' it says to me,
It looks just like the ones on TV!
'No!' I say and say it some more
I hear a click and he blasts down the door.
Laying their unconscious,
Laying there, beaten,
He takes me away
What about my eatin'?

I land on the ship and regain my senses
I meet an alien named Bogalas Genses
He's the top of them all
Although he does remind me of a brick wall . . .
'We come in peace, no trouble at all,
We just want some shoes, 'cause we trip and fall!'
All this commotion, just for shoes.
Aliens! Who knew. . .

Daanyaal Fakier (12)
Dhahran British Grammar School, Saudi Arabia

The Tear From Her Eye!

I walk in the darkness
Staring in despair
I look at the girl over there
With the long black hair.
I walk nearer to her and it starts to get more tense.
I finally start to get more sense.
I walk into more of the darkness,
Creeping even closer.
She turns around, her eyes shining
And there from her gloomy cheek, a tear appears
And falls down her face.
I run away, in a race.

Casey Agland (12)
Dhahran British Grammar School, Saudi Arabia

I Wanna Be Me!

I wanna be different,
I wanna be free.
I don't want any rules
I wanna be me!

I wanna go out
And find my ways.
I wanna stay up all night
And sleep my days.

I wanna come home
And know my work is done,
Go up to my room
And have some fun.

I wanna pop the music,
Dance on my bed.
Not get told off
For not doing what was said.

Don't get me wrong,
Don't misunderstand.
School is cool,
And parents are grand.

I want it all
Grades and fun.

Come on, don't you agree?
Aren't you really just like me?

Samah Ali (11)
Dhahran British Grammar School, Saudi Arabia

School

School is a bore, I hope there is no more,
English is full of punctuation and words.
Maths takes the numbers out of your mouth,
While science blows you away with chemicals.
History is full of gory deeds and death,
While geography is an around the world bore.
DT is all about chopping off fingers
And art is a real moan alisa.
And ICT is all confusion, with all the buttons,
PE is a run-around terror.
French is annoying, with all the pronunciation.
PSE is about dangers of life and helping others.
Music makes you deaf,
And Arabic is full of countries and capitals.

Jack Ball (11)
Dhahran British Grammar School, Saudi Arabia

Ocean Shores

The froth of the pale blue sea
Licks the slanting slope of the sand
And leaves behind little shells,
Left to be taken back again, from the land.

As the sun glistens upon the golden grain
Of the seaside beach.
The young turtles slowly crawl to the shore,
Searching for shelter and protection each.

As the diver jumps into the sea
The water, splashing with joyful glee.
Whilst the newcomer explores his new surroundings,
Once again, the sand meets the sea.

Little ants get showered
As the water clishes, clashes, running as a wanderer in a race.
Along the outskirts of the boundary,
And warming up as the sun flashes
On its frantic face.

As the day ends with a great delight,
The ocean sleeps without a sound.
The fishes swim back into the night.
As the water is now alone, with no one else around.

Miraal Aga (11)
Dhahran British Grammar School, Saudi Arabia

Betrayal

Cold and icy, yet burning and melting inside,
Unexpectedly creeping up upon one's soul,
Climbing, reaching up above,
Plunged inside a heart of fear and sorrow.

The hearts of evil and black,
Will soon come upon those of innocence,
One's life, joy and happiness,
All gone, perished and withered.

If one could turn those hearts to gold,
To soften them to purity and love.
It would take the stars to move from their perfect place,
Up above so high in the sky, so difficult to reach.

That would be an amazing thing to see
To see your hearts so icy and hard.
Melted down as sweet as sugar,
A marvellous change to what will echo, now and forever.

Sara Sheikh (12)
Dhahran British Grammar School, Saudi Arabia

Walk Alone

Up on the roof
Where the sky is blue
I feel for you
But you're not there
I stand looking out to the city
Wallowing in self-pity
Then I go home and think
Next time I say
Will be the day
I walk alone with you.

Grace Tavendale (13)
Dhahran British Grammar School, Saudi Arabia

European Glory

With the head man Rafa,
Otherwise known as the gaffer,
Liverpool won European Cup glory
And here is the amazing story.

In Istanbul on May 25th
Liverpool and AC Milan played a game people could only call a myth,
From 3-0 down to penalty success,
The winners were Liverpool, nobody would have guessed.

Gerrard, Smicer, Alonso, our goal scorers,
This game really failed to bore us.
Instead we were on the edge of our seats
While burning in the blazing heat.

Dudek made amazing saves,
To stop Milan winning, and they were the faves.
So on with the spot-kicks,
I really wondered who Benitez would pick.

When Shevchenko missed the decisive penalty,
The Milan players were crying heavily.
Liverpool players were laughing and dancing,
The commentator was proud, him being Alan Hansen.

Liverpool came home and had a parade,
The players definitely got highly paid,
So that is how we beat Milan
And we're already getting ready for next year's European plan.

Alex Ciesco (12)
Dhahran British Grammar School, Saudi Arabia

Life

Life is exciting and full of happiness,
It's full of amazing adventures,
I love my life as it makes me sing,
That's what I say to almost everything.

If I were truthfully going to say
That life always went my way,
That I love the way my life was going
I'd be lying.

I feel as if my head is spinning,
I feel as if I am dying.
Life has never gone my way
That's what I want to say.

I'm sorry if I sound depressing,
But life isn't as glorious as I thought.
Life is like death, only I'm awake,
And no eternal slumber.

Amy Milner (12)
Dhahran British Grammar School, Saudi Arabia

Can't Trust

It's gone.
It used to be here, but not anymore.
It's taken from us,
We can't do it any more.
So many things are stopping us from believing.
Never stops, wherever you are, it breaks and rips you apart.
We want it and need it. We don't want to live without it.
Just when you think you've got it, it lies and hurts you
More than you can imagine.
It's a shadow,
Something not heard or felt.
It's something we're forgetting.
Something we're still hurting from.
Something we're lacking.
Do you really need it?

Rebecca Louise Nelson (12)
Dhahran British Grammar School, Saudi Arabia

Friendly Foes

'That's not true.'
'I hate you too.'
These are the kind of things said . . .
You get into a fight,
But don't worry, things will be all right,
Things will work out in the end.
You say you won't talk to them, ever again.
Your friendship will eventually mend,
If you say sorry.
Next day you'll be laughing
At the whole scenario and you'll be glad it came to an end.
Sometimes you get in fights,
They sometimes last for nights and nights,
But in the end you will realise how much you miss them.
It shows how delicate a friendship can be,
You have to spend time
Or it will slowly vanish away . . .
Once it's gone, it's hard to get the same friendship back,
You'll miss the laughs,
The good times you had.
And you will regret the time you didn't spend with them.
'It wasn't *my* fault.'
'*You* say sorry, it was *your* fault.'
Always avoid these things to say,
Do what you can to make things right.
If that's not enough then it's not worth it.
Say you're sorry, let's start over,
And good things will come your way!

Rose Maunder (13)
Dhahran British Grammar School, Saudi Arabia

Death

It creeps through your door while you're sleeping,
Its breath, as cold as ice.
One kiss and you're paralysed,
Too stiff to move, too stiff to breathe.
Never to return to this cruel place we call home,
As you wither in pain, a happy smile forms on your face.
Another new soul it thinks, another new heart.
What is this creature, you may wonder?
'Tis death.
It creeps through your door when you're sleeping,
And with one kiss, you're gone . . .

Sophia Hodgkinson (12)
Dhahran British Grammar School, Saudi Arabia

Tiger, Tiger

Tiger, tiger in the tree,
Looking down at me.
I try to run, I try to hide,
I don't know what's going through his mind.
Tiger, tiger in the tree.

His stripes are orange
His stripes are white,
His eyes are amber and very bright.

He ran away to find something to eat,
To hunt and search for his meat.
I thought that he would make me his treat.
Tasty fingers and delicious feet.
Tiger, tiger in the tree.

Mahmood Dayaji (14)
Dhahran British Grammar School, Saudi Arabia

The Castle

The castle stands alone
On the hill
Evil forces wish you ill.

Oppressive silence fills
The air,
No one's there.

The shadows cast their patterns
On the walls that saw it all.
Love, hate and tragedy,
The greatest powers rise and fall.

Years of life and death there
Left their mark upon the stone.
How many people have deserted
This cold and lonely home?

People come and people go,
Battles lost and won.
Time gone and past, walls built to last,
The ending has begun.

Lives lost, lives found and lives commence
Where dead and living meet,
In this place upon the hill
Our hearts as one will beat.

Holly Carberry (14)
Dhahran British Grammar School, Saudi Arabia

The Dark Night

Dark nights tend to show the things you never want to see,
Unprotected from the unknown,
It's not going to surprise me,
For my life is a dream
But I always notice a blue moon in the night sky,
Convincing me this is not real,
But actually a lie.

I stare at the sky with confusion,
Mixed emotions in my head.
Counting the stars just to help me think,
Thinking of what life holds in store for me.

Falling asleep,
Dreaming of the dark starless sky
Introduces me to reality
Meaning no more lies.
When the sun rises in the sky,
I awake for no reason.
I cannot say what happened that night
For I do not want to remember.

The dark night is dangerous,
It is like a disguise
To hide my truth and others' lies.

Anastasia Clarke (13)
Dhahran British Grammar School, Saudi Arabia

Imagine

Imagine, imagine a world without war,
Where there is no need for violence anymore,
Everyone living in peace and harmony,
Imagine there is more money for everyone to share
No need for greed or any despair.
Imagine there are cures for every illness and disease,
Everyone's life span will increase,
Imagine that everyone is equal.
No one is superior, everyone is the same,
Would this be better or would it be lame.
Imagine that the world turned upside down,
Would it just keep spinning, round and round?
Imagine, imagine what will happen next?
No one knows, so you will just have to guess.

Jackie Tang (13)
Dhahran British Grammar School, Saudi Arabia

Tag

Eyes in the mirror
A foot on the stairs
Legs out the door
Someone who's not there

A flash of a smile
On the way to school
A hand up high
Making me feel a fool

Once I'm home
A shadow I see
Am I insane to think
That someone's following me?

As I lie in bed
I look up to see
Smiling evilly
A thing, glaring at me

A djinn unknown
A demon from Hell
Will this day be marked
As the day I fell?

I played tag with a ghost
Every night down the lane
And for some reason
People think I'm insane.

Tabassum Fakier (13)
Dhahran British Grammar School, Saudi Arabia

Ocean

Ocean wide so blue and deep,
Where sharks and fish and lobsters creep.
Lurking in the seaweed bed,
Or between the coral lumps instead.

Shells are scattered on the ground,
Moving sea life is the only sound.
Whales are eating tiny krill,
While great white sharks seek their kill.

Fishermen try to catch cod,
As dolphins play games in a pod.
They leap and jump from wave to wave,
Divers search an underwater cave.

Ocean wide so blue and deep,
Where sharks and fish and lobsters creep.

Natalie Ciesco (14)
Dhahran British Grammar School, Saudi Arabia

The Silver Screen

It all just seems so easy as I'm sitting in my seat,
A structured plot, (though moves a lot) and one fantastic fête
A hero who wades through the story - start, beginning, end
Captured in the magic, in a world where all hearts mend
It all just seems so perfect real life struggles to contend.

Then the closing curtain draws, and I'm alone in a stiff seat
In a dark room, truth's blunt gloom, envelopes me like a sheet
The outside street feels dull without the movie's polished sheen
An open space with no subtitles stating to you what they mean
Makes me wonder if my life would look better through a screen.

And though it seems to some that this perfection is disturbing
It brings to light, through daily plight, the dreary woes we're curbing
So perhaps our own life's movie may boast no terrific cast
We know without a running time ours doesn't slip so fast
It helps me to remember, nothing perfect hopes to last.

Hadeel Mohamed (14)
Dhahran British Grammar School, Saudi Arabia

Coming

They are coming; you should run before the time runs out.
They come with obsession only, to hear the people scream
                                    and shout
They are coming; it's the start of another cold and death-filled night
They will destroy us, they will break us, they see no wrong
                                    or right.
They are coming . . .

Do you hear the drums beating with the rhythm of our passion?
Do you hear the drums pounding in your ears in a dreadful fashion?
Can you hear the drums thumping with a pulse of its own being?
Can you hear the drums vibrating, reflecting all you're seeing?
They are coming . . .

Do you see the warriors dancing with their bare chests around
                                    the fire?
Do you see the sweat that's glinting, resulting from their desire?
Can you see the moon rising with fearful premonitions?
Can you see the anxious faces, trying to make decisions?
They are coming . . .

Do you feel the power of the clan coming together?
Do you feel the darkness rising, smothering their lives forever?
Can you feel the pulsing of the fear throughout their veins?
Can you feel the regret at the arriving grief and pain?
They are coming . . .

They are coming, getting closer, bringing chaos and despair
They are coming, getting nearer . . .
They are here.

Samantha Botha (13)
Dhahran British Grammar School, Saudi Arabia

Senses

Fear looks like the red of a bush fire.
Fear feels like the cold, slippery banks of a river at night.
Fear smells like gunpowder.
Fear tastes like milk that has gone sour.
Fear sounds like the screams of a dying animal.

Darkness looks like the howl of a wolf at night.
Darkness feels like the icy cold water of a lake at night.
Darkness smells of nothing: it is a blank thing.
Darkness tastes like sour worms.
Darkness sounds like nothing: it is blank and scary.

Jaco Langenhoven (14)
Dhahran British Grammar School, Saudi Arabia

Dreams

Listen to your dreams,
Listen to your dreams that come from your heart,
Listen to your dreams that come from your mind,
But most of all,
Listen to those that come from your soul,
Those are the dreams,
Dreams where you have it all.

Ali Ersoz (15)
Dhahran British Grammar School, Saudi Arabia

I Can't Think Of A Title For It

Sitting, trying to write a poem
I think to myself *come on, you gotta get goin'*
I'm stuck for words
I can't think at all
I look at the time and try to stall.

I look out the window and see the sky
It isn't very blue, I wonder why
I stare at the wall
Is this supposed to rhyme?
I have so much trouble keeping it in time.

Hold on, look how much I've done
Hey, it was even kind of fun
Wait, two lines to go.

Hayley Brown (14)
Dhahran British Grammar School, Saudi Arabia

Survivor

Thirty-nine days to outwit, outplay and outlast,
The season has begun with a brand new cast.

Split into tribes, with strangers and unity,
This possibly assists them to win immunity.

Shelter is made with whatever they can seek,
Food is rationed, which makes them become weak.

Crocodiles and piranhas inhabit the lakes,
But then again, one million dollars is at stake.

Gruelling, demanding challenges, with many rewards,
Chances of a lifetime, all in an hour's show.

But when they lose, alliances start to form,
Lying, back stabbing and strong bonds are torn.

As the night goes, someone leaves heartbroken,
After Jeff Probst remarks, 'The tribe has spoken.'

Fowzia Mahmood (14)
Dhahran British Grammar School, Saudi Arabia

Ode To Chicken And Ice Cream

Here is a comparison between chicken and ice cream
One tastes well, like chicken, the other a dream
One is healthier or so mothers say
But I disagree, I'd rather have sweets every day.

One has been born, probably on some farm
Or has it been modified with needles and harm?
It can be roasted to a crispy delight
The other is just laughable to see it alight.

Have you ever heard of toasted ice cream?
Have you ever had it fried, or had it steamed
Or thrown into a barbecue to sit and grill?
Watching as it blazes. Oh what a thrill!

Have you ever noticed that chicken does surround us?
Frog legs, spider eggs, fish, snails and octopus
All taste remarkably like *chicken!*
Chicken! Chicken! Chicken!

But then there's ice cream, a food group in itself
So many flavours just sitting on the shelf
How can I decide between mint chocolate chip
Or maybe if I desire a bit of caramel whip
Or if I fancy a tang of rainbow swirl
Tickle me pink and jump and twirl?

Please don't get me wrong, I've got nothing against chicken
Only that ice cream is much more finger lickin'!
But if I persist and make it my life goal
Chicken flavoured ice cream may one day be sold!

Hager Haggag (14)
Dhahran British Grammar School, Saudi Arabia

Happy Time

This is the thing that brings you joy,
This is better than any toy.

This is the thing that makes you smile,
For this thing you'd run a mile.

This is the thing that brings delight
The greatest thing to cross my sight.

This is the thing of which dreams are made,
The pleasure of this will never fade.

This is the finest thing known to man,
It's eating time during Ramadan.

Danyaal Hamdani (14)
Dhahran British Grammar School, Saudi Arabia

Life

Five days a week are the same
The other two are just a game.
I see the same people most of the time,
But I wish I could see you all the time.

I argue with my parents about school
Sometimes I just look like a fool.
They will never understand what I mean
So I just keep living in this dream.

I don't know where life will take me
I just hope it doesn't break me
And if it does,
You'll be there to save me . . .

Chris Morris (15)
Dhahran British Grammar School, Saudi Arabia

Message In A Bottle

With her womanly figure
She stands staring at me
Her curves so rare
It's easy to see.

Filled with sweetness
She stands calling for me
Reaching to touch her
So she could be free.

I must get her before it's too late
As the kids will be home by half-past eight
There's no one like her . . . Coca-Cola . . . enjoy!

Safia Mohamed (16)
Dhahran British Grammar School, Saudi Arabia

Pointless Questions

What does it mean,
That symbol I wrote down,
        But now forgotten?

What is the reason,
They gathered in the empty house,
        Carrying only candles?

I don't understand why I am left alone,
Always talking to myself as I imagine.
I feel I am never home.

Why is he there,
Every day when it is dark,
Sitting in the tree,
        And staring at the sky?

Who will I become,
If I stay in this place,
A waste of nothingness
        That surrounds me?

There are no answers to my questions
        Who, what, where or why?

Rumana Mahmood (15)
Dhahran British Grammar School, Saudi Arabia

Seasons Change

Silvery moon glistening at her
        Reflecting upon her beautiful face
Across the twinkling river . . .

        Arms spread out, free from her side
Gentle wind stroking her hair smoothly
        A princess enjoying her faraway ride . . .

So who is this lady?
        Who could she be?
Looking over the ocean, green eyes
        Orange slightly . . .

I guess she's there for a reason
        Arms spread out, set free from her side
She'll only change with the season . . .

Reem Masri (15)
Dhahran British Grammar School, Saudi Arabia

The Cheetah And The Springbuck

Stealthy and fast is the cheetah
Chasing its prey in the open plains
Dodging trees and jumping bushes
This big cat is built for speed.

It kills its prey with jaws and claws
After a chase that is over in seconds
Very fast with camouflage of yellow fur and black spots.

Its favourite food is the springbuck
With strong legs it leaps into the air
But is no match for the cheetah
Travelling at speeds of 70km an hour
This is the fastest land animal.

Matthew Barber (14)
Dhahran British Grammar School, Saudi Arabia

Him Who Was Me . . .

Hand in hand we walk,
A walk on the beach,
On its polished silky sand.

Where the waves collide,
And give the biggest of the dash
Where the sun meets the deep
And gives the brightest of the spark.

Whenever I see her,
Her features,
Her face,
Her smile,
I feel the sun is shining on me.

There can't be anything superior,
Not even near.
But then it all fell back,
Everything turned black,
I felt swallowed by Hell.

When she said
She did not love him,
Who was me.

She had moved out on me.
The affectionate light in the darkness of my life had gone,
It felt darker and dimmer for eternity.
My heart ice-covered to its core,
And from here I did not want to breath any more.

Saad Khan Malik (13)
Dhahran British Grammar School, Saudi Arabia

Betrayed

I have lost that beauty that glowed so bright,
And the joys of security with cries of delight.
Hopes now drown in the greedy eyes of sorrow,
I'd bear false to hope for a sweet tomorrow.

Memories arise from the graves of my mind,
Casting out peace, I so long to find.
This heart swells like an ungroomed cut,
Leaving all doors of expectation firmly shut.

Bitterness indulges me, now my only friend,
The bands of friendship entangled to no end.
For in your bandage of trust, my life was laid,
But Shelley, you've left . . . so I stand betrayed.

Jasmin Jade Nunn (14)
Dhahran British Grammar School, Saudi Arabia

Homework

Homework, homework, it's a crying shame,
Every day it's the same old game.

I come back home thinking work is over,
Wanna put my feet up on the sofa.

A startling voice says, 'To your room,'
Happiness taken away too soon.

I hit my desk in a miserable mood,
And there I stay until it's time for food.

What gives parents the right to tell us,
Why to make homework such a big fuss?

Why don't they realise where I wanna be?
Yeah, you guessed it, I wanna be free.

My friends are waiting for me to go out,
So I guess I better give up the shout.

I knuckle down, buckle down, do the stuff,
Now, I've finished, I've had enough.

I don't wanna go back, start from scratch,
I wish I was an egg, I'd never hatch.

Karim Ali (13)
Dhahran British Grammar School, Saudi Arabia

Your Treasure

A true friend is your treasure
Hard to find
But precious to gain
He's always beside you
To share your moments
Ready to listen with a sympathetic ear
Always understanding and caring
And always forgetting your mistakes
That's your true friend
That you shall never lose.

Mariam Elbadrashini (13)
Dhahran British Grammar School, Saudi Arabia

Unsure

Don't know how to get there,
Don't know who to see,
Don't know what I'll do there,
Don't know if I need a key,
Don't know if it's nice there,
Don't know if it's scary,
All I know is I'm leaving now,
Would you like to join me?

Dakota Harper (14)
Dhahran British Grammar School, Saudi Arabia

A Poem About Nothing

People will ask you to write.
They will ask you to write about books or trees,
Or the way human nature is.
I cannot so I will write about nothing.
Nothing is a word that means everything.
It's what a child will say to his mother,
When he is caught next to the empty cookie jar.
Or what a schoolboy will say to his parents when they
Ask why he has not done his homework again.

Josh said nothing a lot,
He said nothing to his teacher,
When the children were laughing at him,
And he said nothing when they locked him in
The school basement for a night
He also said nothing when his father hit him
Again and again for being late
And pushed him into the wall.

He also said nothing when he walked to
The top of the tallest building,
But when he jumped he did say something
. . . 'Help!'

EJ Thompson-Hall (14)
Dhahran British Grammar School, Saudi Arabia

Beautiful Stranger

I love the way you walk,
The way you flick your hair.
The way you always smile,
I can't help but stare.
Beautiful stranger.

I love your gorgeous style,
And your sparkling brown eyes,
I gave up approaching you,
I've had too many tries.
Beautiful stranger.

I love that you're so kind,
And greet everyone so sweetly,
The way you are, the way you dress,
Forever displayed neatly.
Beautiful stranger.

I love the way you always look cheerful,
And never ever frown,
Not even the worst of news,
Could ever pull you down.
Beautiful stranger.

I love the way you giggle,
And laugh with your friends,
I love the way you care about appearance,
In with all new trends,
Beautiful stranger.

If only I could come into your life,
Reach in and take your hand,
Live happily in love,
Our names engraved in sand.
You're a beautiful stranger.

Natasha Gibbons (15)
Dhahran British Grammar School, Saudi Arabia

South Africa

South Africa is my home,
Where the Rainbow Nation is.
There are many different cities,
Jo'burg, Durban, Cape Town.
The terrain is very different
With sea, mountains and the plains
Cape Point, Table Mountain and the Karoo.
All the different types of people,
The eleven languages that we speak,
Make up this wonderful land.
The rural area is so bare,
The urban is too crowded.
Different climates, hot and cold,
Windy and calm, dry and wet.
The animals are the best,
Rhino, elephant, lion, buffalo and the leopard.
These are what make my home.

Jenny Armstrong (14)
Dhahran British Grammar School, Saudi Arabia

Life

Life is a journey through the forests
You forget your path on the way
You expect something new after every step
And you lose hope when it gets dark.

Tall, towering trees block your journey
Just like your enemies and rivals,
Owls hooting in the night-time
Much like friends and loved ones who support you.

A constant, continuous trail throughout the woods
Resembling your youth, prime and old age.
In the morning, blossoming flower beds that are new,
Exactly like many happy memories behind you.

Mirza Sameer Beg (14)
Dhahran British Grammar School, Saudi Arabia

Gone

Your caring yet wrinkled hands touched my baby soft skin
Held me as I crawled on this Earth
Your curiosity indulged me as I peered around
Your expression didn't need words
The warm sunny smile of yours shone upon me.

Why couldn't I talk to you? Though I longed to do so.
Why couldn't I ask how are you? Though I yearned to do so.
Why couldn't I spend my lfe with you? Though I wished to do so.

Your tears ripped my heart open
As I left, why couldn't your eyes open?
Did time stop for you and me? No, it didn't.

I raise these hands of mine (which you embraced before)
Pray to God for your cure, no use for medicine anymore
'Mira, your grandma is . . . '
It struck me that everything is falling to unwanted pieces,
'. . . ill again.'
My eyes open to a dark road with a shine far, far ahead.

I try to reach that shine as if it was my life,
Stretch my arms as far as I could,
But darkness filled that light,
As I receive a message,
'She's gone.'

Fatin Amirah Bakar (15)
Dhahran British Grammar School, Saudi Arabia

An Empty Space

Pitch-black darkness engulfs me,
It's like the loneliness . . . the emptiness in my life,
I can hear the clock, tick . . . tick no faster, no slower,
As if time itself is going to face its death.

A dog faces me as I look out of the window,
Its eyes pleading and innocent, staring at me with hope.
I look away, hiding my tears,
From the dog, from life, from my mind.

I feel suffocated within myself,
It feels like the light of happiness will never dance upon me.
I look at myself in the mirror to see a helpless person
With eyes that hold back waterfalls of hurt.

As I look deep into my eyes,
I feel myself getting lost into a trance,
As though I don't even recognise myself.
An expressionless face with trapped desires and emotions.

I hear the trees rustling outside,
The traffic roars past,
The sun shines brightly, with children laughing,
People of all ages swarm the streets.

But still there is no one to help me,
No one to share their tears with me,
No one to cuddle me in their warm arms.
It's like the loneliness . . . the emptiness in my life.

Aishwarya Shetty
Dhahran British Grammar School, Saudi Arabia

My Friends

My friends are cool
They always play pool.

They cheer me up when I am down
They make me laugh when we go to town.

They always love me and I will always love them
But they might hate me when I hurt them.

Friends may come, friends may go
But these friends will last so long.

Sally Hamilton (13)
Dhahran British Grammar School, Saudi Arabia

Love

Love is my life
Love is your life.

I breathe it in
You breathe it out.

We stick together
Like flowers, like bees.

As long as I'm sweet
Stick with me!

Paloma Lauder (13)
Dhahran British Grammar School, Saudi Arabia

The Sun

The sun is what gives us life
The sun is what gives us light
The sun is what gives us warmth
The sun is what gives us energy
The sun is what gives us happiness
The sun is what gives us plants
The sun is what gives us growth
The sun is what gives us . . . cancer.

The sun gives us everything we need in life
We could not live without the sun
Every year it pulls us closer into its fiery grasp
The sun is the source of life and death alike.

Alex Lewis (12)
Dhahran British Grammar School, Saudi Arabia

Old Times

When I was younger I could slide through mud, play on swings
And do whatever I wanted to do.

I remember when I went out just before a party,
When I was 8 and my dad said don't get dirty
And I started sliding in mud to get dirty
And I got dragged to the party covered in mud,
I didn't slide in mud again.

But now I am older,
I have to take my own responsibility.

I wish I could go back in time,
To the good old days,
They were so much fun,
But I can't go back in time.

It would be a dream come true,
If I could go back in time.

Deri Lloyd (12)
Dhahran British Grammar School, Saudi Arabia

The Beach

Walking along the beach at night
Watching the sun go down.

Listening to the seagulls
With my feet in the ground.

Picking up pebble stones
To skip along the sea.

Listening to the waves
Sway back at me.

Watching people walk their dogs
Throwing frisbees as they jog.

People have gone, silence now,
The moon is bright, stars are out.

Going home.

Keely Peters (12)
Dhahran British Grammar School, Saudi Arabia

My Wakeboard

I went wakeboarding one amazing day
And saw some wicked things,
Like dolphins skiing on some jellyfish
And squids doing flips
And if that's not really enough
I saw some swordfish mono skiing
But when I got back
No one would believe me.

Ryan Allen (11)
Dhahran British Grammar School, Saudi Arabia

Creatures Of Redwall Beware, Beware!

Creatures of Redwall beware, beware
Beware of what lies in Mossflower wood
With six big eyes and chains for tails.
Creatures of Redwall beware, beware
They hunt for food night and day
And eat it alive or dead
With fangs full of deadly poison
And breath that smells of sewage.
Creatures of Redwall beware, beware
They'll slither behind you
And raise their heads
Open their mouths
And take you away.
Creatures of Redwall beware, beware
Beware of the trio snakes!

Laila Uba (11)
Dhahran British Grammar School, Saudi Arabia

Shades Of Grey

Black, black, the skies are black.
Blue, blue, my life is blue.
Brown, brown, the trees are brown.
Green, green, why aren't they green?
The world is being polluted by uncaring people
Oh how I wish for the world to be a better place.
Green, green, for the trees to be green.
The ground, the ground, for the ground to not be polluted.
Sea, sea, for the sea to be crystal clear;
But for now shades of grey are the colours I see.

Daniel Smith (11)
Dhahran British Grammar School, Saudi Arabia

Young Writers - POP! International Inspirations

Blue

Blue is a very important colour,
It is what we feel when we are sick,
When we are weak,
When we are sad.

There are shades of blue,
Soft baby blue,
Shocking electric blue,
High sky-blue,
Slippery ice-blue,
Fuzzy velvet blue,
And dazzling dark blue.

Blue is the colour of,
Eyes,
Your lips when they're cold,
Bluebirds,
Dolphins' skin.

Without blue we would have
Colourless waves,
Black emotions
And yellow birds.

Parish Minton (11)
Dhahran British Grammar School, Saudi Arabia

Getting Ready For School

Alarm goes off,
Don't want to go to school.
Mum comes in,
Pulls off covers,
Don't want to go to school.

Slowly down the stairs,
Brother and sister eating,
Don't want to go to school.
Had breakfast,
Got dressed,
Don't want to go to school.

Mum makes lunch,
You pack bag,
Don't want to go to school.
Watch TV,
Don't want to go to school.

Get to the bus,
Sit down, go to sleep,
Don't want to go to school.
At school,
First class,
Don't want to go to school.

I just
Don't want to go to school!

Rhiannon Smith (11)
Dhahran British Grammar School, Saudi Arabia

My Best Friend

He came and spoke to me when I was down
He said, 'Hey don't frown
What's the matter?
Please don't make a clatter.'
My best friend

He invited me to his house
'Don't be silly, you're like a mouse.'
We played and played and played all day
His butler said, 'Time to go I say.'
My best friend

In school the next day
He said, 'Oh Jimmy
I need to tell you something.'
My heart was drumming
Not my best friend

I was wandering around school
A boy said, 'Hey that looks cool.'
He looked at my mobile and we started talking
Next thing you knew we started walking
My best friend.

Zeshan Hussein (13)
Dhahran British Grammar School, Saudi Arabia

You're My All

How I don't know, but you complete my soul.
Angel, yes you are, such a beautiful shooting star.
Blissful and gifted, you're my lucky charm.
I could worship those brown eyes; they shine right through me,
wherever you are
Beautiful, brave and bright when I see you, I can't get you
out of my sight
Amazingly adorable, I don't know how to explain.
Love and its great gifts, its power, its music, how it drives us insane
But with you it's different, a shining sweet smile
and an understanding mind
I just love you; you're my all and one of a kind.

Nora Mawla (15)
Dhahran British Grammar School, Saudi Arabia

Hungary

I am from a country where nobody else is from,
I am from a country that British people dream of coming from,
If anyone knows anything about it,
Then they do not want to talk about it.
My country has the Balaton Lake,
It is a very nice place to have a break,
If you've ever been to Budapest,
You know that it is a good place to have a rest.
If you have a chance,
Feel free to go and have a rest!

Mark Szoboszlay (14)
Dhahran British Grammar School, Saudi Arabia

Born To Better The World

(This poem is dedicated to cultism)

We all were born to move the world
Not to be moved by the world
Born to better the world
Not to be battered by the world.

Cultism, the faceless sorrow
Harrowing our dreams as a hero
The Lucifer's lieutenant
Making our visions impotent.

Why do we slaughter our brothers
Like a captive of callous robbers
Defiling the purity of our sisters
Only to call ourselves brothers?

We must divorce cultism
And be bride to patriotism
Cultism, a captivity that lasts eternally
Fretting his victims with the freckles of vanity
Our dreams could be achieved in a better way
With our sorrows and fears all gone astray
Making for us a peaceful Earth
As peaceful as the Sabbath.

Let's show the world a better us
Let's turn the world a peaceful universe
Cultism destroys the me that makes me, me
Living in a sorrowful state, that innocent me
We must shun the spirit of cultism
And embrace heroism and patriotism
So together we would sing in unity
The lullaby of peace for eternity.

Akhenemhen Lucky (17)
International School Ibadan, Nigeria

Funny Poem

When everyone was bored and the sky was grey
And my dad had no good games to play,
We sat down on the grass feeling really low
And began to think why life was so slow.
And there in the distance beyond and beyond
We saw Jake's granpa fall in the pond.
We were tickled with delight
Because Granpa really was not so bright.
We ran for the camera oh so quick,
So when Jake's granpa got out, *click, click, click.*
I don't think Granpa was quick to respond
But it was funny when Jake's granpa fell in the pond.

Alexander Francis (11)
The English International College, Spain

The Sea

The sea, the sea,
What a wonderful place to be!
Dolphins swimming,
Mermaids grinning,
Oh! what a wonderful place to be!
Gliding in and out of the place,
I love it, don't you?
Oh! what glee!
Swimming with my family and me,
Jumping and curving,
Gliding and swerving,
I love being a fish,
Except, I have one nightmare,
Being fried and put on a dish!

Ellie McCarthy (11)
The English International College, Spain

My Poem-Kin

They roll at night,
Eyes like moonlight,
Their wicked grin,
The light is dim.

The one green hair,
Their heads are bare,
With triangular eyes,
The reason of lies.

Sweets on the floor,
Knocks on the door,
With 'monsters' on the streets,
There are lots of ghouls to greet.

Jeroen Rijks (8)
The English International College, Spain

Haunted Poem

It's a cold and dark winter night,
The young boy is lost and no one is in sight,
The trees shiver and the forest feels spooky,
Something is creeping behind him, it is so freaky.

He screams and starts to run away,
But in front of him a strange shape comes into play,
He jumps back thinking it's a ghost
And all panicked he says to himself, 'I'm toast.'

The sky above his head fills up with lightning,
The scene around him gets more and more frightening,
Confusion and fear are mixed up in his mind,
He doesn't know where to hide, he feels blind.

He races wildly looking for an escape,
Wondering if he is being followed by that strange shape,
He finally succeeds in getting out of this horrible place
And there in front of him is his mum's welcoming face.

Joseph El Khoury (11)
The English International College, Spain

The Window

As I looked outside the window
Of the quiet room
All I saw was rain,
All I felt was gloom.

No smily faces outside,
No bright light shining on the trees,
I saw nothing I liked,
There was nothing I could see.

No little children
Playing on the streets,
I just looked out there
Sitting on my seat.

As I looked outside the window
Of the quiet room
All I saw was rain,
All I felt was gloom.

Paige Hopkins (13)
The English International College, Spain

Angel To Devil

So sweet
So innocent
So good
So pretty and fine
Angel to devil.
Angel to devil in a split second
So mean
So bad
Such evilness
So much power stuck inside her
Angel to devil.
No friends
No family
No one to talk to
She's all alone
Angel to devil.
Help this poor child
She has two sets of feelings
Some good, some bad
Angel to devil.

Emily Alexander (12)
The English International College, Spain

The White Light

The white light
behind the door
that shines so bright,
that comes before the war.

The white light
laying on the ground
gave me a fright
and made my heart pound.

The white light
coming around the corner
came at night,
made the air as hot as a sauna.

The white light
as bright as the sun
made my head look right,
that made me run.

The white light
that brought children's smiles
and looked like an angel in their sight
carried on for miles and miles.

Alexandra Burchett (11)
The English International College, Spain

Running

The tense atmosphere surrounds you,
Suddenly you don't know what to do,
The bang goes off and you start to fuss,
Everyone's cheering and you're in a rush!

You start to sprint but you start to slow,
The others gather speed, suddenly you feel low,
You see the finish line ahead and focus on it,
Oh no! Your legs start to ache and you just want to sit.
But as quick as a wink you cross the line,
You're first, yes! Goodbye!

Lucy Gardner (11)
The English International College, Spain

Scary House

Late at night when you're sleeping
That's when creatures come a-creeping.

To your house these creatures slither
Making sounds that make you shiver.

Scratching on your windowpane
Whispering your own first name.

Tapping on the nearest door
Creaking stairs and floors and more.

Making you sit up in bed
Or pull the covers over your head.

And whilst you sit there filled with fear
You wish your grampa Bob was near.

Sirage Saudi (11)
The English International College, Spain

Gibraltar

One year ago
My parents said, 'Let's go!
We're going to Gibraltar to see the monkeys play,
While we drink a Fanta in a very good café.'

We took a while to get there, there was a traffic jam,
In the car I was eating a sandwich made of ham.
My brother Jorge was complaining about the journey,
He nearly vomited on me!

We were going up the mountain, when we got to the top,
There was a massive rock,
Over the rock we looked and we saw a group of boats,
It was very cold so we put on our coats.

In the car we loaded our sack,
We were on our way back.
During the journey back (which was much better),
I took off my sweater!

Juan Prieto (11)
The English International College, Spain

My Haunted Day

Unless you are the craziest man,
You would never go to this place,
Which I remember very well,
As clear as a face.

If you would ever go there,
You would be haunted for life
And have horrible nightmares,
Of being chased by a knife.

When I was there I was chased by skeletons,
Which could run at great haste,
I knew that if they caught me,
They would kill me with swords at their waist.

Then there's a monster in there,
Though just why I cannot tell
And although I couldn't see it,
It could see me well.

Oh my heart was beating faster,
Faster than a drum,
For all I heard was its footsteps
And my body was frozen numb.

Then I ran and ran as fast as I could
And hoped to reach the door,
But then hands started to grab me,
Which came out of the floor.

After struggling and struggling I finally got up
And staggered out the door in pain,
Then as I walked out of the gates I knew,
I would never go there again!

Max Burrows (11)
The English International College, Spain

Through And Through

Friends, friends are always there,
Friends, friends to like and care,
Friends, friends help you through,
Friends, friends through and through.

Parents, parents always nag,
Parents, parents pack your bag,
Parents, parents love you true,
Parents, parents through and through.

Teachers, teachers are all mean,
Teachers, teachers are really keen,
Teachers, teachers love helping you,
Teachers, teachers through and through.

George Gibson (12)
The English International College, Spain

I Want, I Want

I want, I want a PSP,
If I'm lucky I will get three,
If I don't I will give up.

I want, I want someone who
Could do my homework,
Then I could play with my friends.

I want, I want a caring mother
That will be there by my side,
I'm lucky, she always is.

I want, I want to achieve my sports,
If I could I certainly would,
That will be my dream.

Kent Margison (11)
The English International College, Spain

This Is War

This is war!
You pinch my powder and dust your face,
And throw my jewellery all over the place.
'Don't take my lipstick, it isn't your colour.
If you do it again I am telling Mother.'
War I tell you!
I know you're my only brother,
But I would swap you for another.
You go through my diary and show the whole school,
You're a total pain, but you think you are so cool.
You think life is all fun and games,
But I am sick of getting the blame.
This is certainly war!

Rhyanna Owen (12)
The English International College, Spain

My Advice Poem To A New Kid

Before the first day of school
You have to learn this rule.
Before getting into strife
Read this for a good life.

Before picking on teachers
Be sure they aren't creatures.
Before teachers tell you off
Try not to make them cross.

Before lending equipment
Make sure you have consent.
Before doing your homework
Make sure your pen does work.

Before buying a big lunch
On which you'd want to much.
Before losing your money
The prices aren't funny.

Before having lots of mates
Hope you have at least eight.
Before tucking out your shirt
Friends could say it's a skirt.

Even though you might be scared
Now I'm sure you're prepared.

Bryan De Bruyne (13)
The English International College, Spain

Advice To A New Kid

Beware of big Steve,
Don't think to cross his path.
Beware of Miss Jones
For she can't have a laugh.

Beware of the prefect
He thinks he's in charge.
Beware the caretaker,
He's always at large.

Beware of the head
Because he makes the rules.
Beware of buildings
That are known as schools!

Alex Maybrey (12)
The English International College, Spain

Advice To A Would-Be Smoker

Fact or fiction, true or false
You're the one to decide.
Smoking is fun,
It's chic and cool,
An efficient means of weight control
And quite obviously not addictive,
An indispensable social skill
And excellent stress buster,
What could be healthier?
A smoking stick to nicotine stain
The fingers, nails and teeth.
A single source of nourishment,
Countless broken New Year's resolutions,
Banned in the office and public places,
A full day's work for a 10 minute drag,
Your perception is your reality.

Alicia May Dean (12)
The English International College, Spain

Advice To A New Kid

Beware of the bullies
As they might steal your money
Which is annoying
And not very funny.
If you get bullied
Don't just stand there and be scared,
Stand up for yourself
And make them care
About you and everyone else!
There is always a bully around
Who tells everyone to not make a sound.

Kim Wehmeyer (13)
The English International College, Spain

The Monstrous Teacher

Beware of the teacher,
It is a very evil creature.
It lurks in the dark,
Waiting for you to bark,
'I haven't done my homework.'
Then it will turn around and look into your eyes,
Then quickly a rope around you it will tie
And hang you up real high,
Waiting for you to die . . .

Philip Blau (12)
The English International College, Spain

My Advice To A New Kid

Beware of your image
When you first come to school
Or otherwise your friends and enemies will bully you.
Beware of the teachers
In case you did not know,
For they are known as awful creatures.
Beware of your shirt,
If it is not tucked in
The principal will ask you to wear a skirt.
This could happen when you come to my school
And if you're lucky they might be nice to you,
Just because you're new.

Mike Tervoort (13)
The English International College, Spain

You Don't Want To Be Older!

Being older isn't great,
There's a lot more stuff you have to do
That you'll hate,
Take it from me.

There's a lot of responsibilities
Like looking after your bro or sis,
Or not losing your keys,
Don't grow up!

Way more chores to do,
Some disgusting things
Like cleaning the loo,
Don't grow up!

So don't try to act older than your age,
Stop going through your mum's make-up,
Doesn't matter that you're missing parties that are the rage,
That you are too young to go to.

So if you think getting older
Is the best,
Think about it again
And give it a rest.

Veronika Kotetishvili (12)
The English International College, Spain

I've Forgotten

I've forgotten, I've forgotten
My first ELC teacher.
I've forgotten, I've forgotten,
Was she a fierce creature?

I remember, I remember
My first day in secondary.
I remember, I remember
Emilio tried to make friends with me.

I've forgotten, I've forgotten
How big was the room?
I've forgotten, I've forgotten,
I hope to go back there soon.

I remember, I remember
The playground was great.
I remember, I remember
Playing with my best mate.

Joshua Kenyon (11)
The English International College, Spain

I Remember, I Remember!

I remember, I remember
My first day of secondary,
I felt horrified and fearful.
I remember, I remember
Faces asking me what my name is,
Where I'm from now and how old I am.
I remember, I remember
Writing words I've never heard before,
Suddenly the bell rang hardly.
I remember, I remember
Walking down to my next classroom,
When we went in, I was all alone.
I remember, I remember
Putting my hand up to ask questions,
As I said a word, I froze with fear.
I remember, I remember
A girl asking me if I was fine,
I muttered, 'Yes, I'm fine thank you.'
I remember, I remember
Looking at the clock to see the time,
Hoping it's the end of the lesson.
I remember, I remember
Hearing scraping chairs gossip
And the teacher telling boys off.
I remember, I remember
Having tears dripping from my eyes
And I was eager to get home!

Lucy Butler (12)
The English International College, Spain

The Thing I Can't Explain

I can't explain this feeling,
I can't explain this way,
I just cannot understand,
This very special day.

Sometimes I just can't get it,
It's hard to let it go,
This feeling which wants to make me cry,
I really do not know.

Sometimes I hear this voice,
Calling out my name,
It really starts to scare me,
This isn't a fun game.

It could be a lost spirit,
Waiting for some hope,
It could also be my bunny,
Pulling on Heaven's rope.

Please thing that I can't explain,
Please don't let me die,
I want to ask a final time,
Why, is it *your* helpless cry?

Yasmeen Abusakout (11)
The English International College, Spain

Family Bonds

Stay together for the kids,
For the happy look upon their face,
Do it for the kids
And hope they live in a happier place.

Remember your kids
When you fight and disagree,
Just look at your kids
And all the bad things they have to see.

Think about their future
And all the things they could do,
Become a doctor, a lawyer,
Maybe famous too.

Stay together for the kids,
They have dreams too,
Stay together for the kids
And maybe their dreams will come true.

Rory Williamson (12)
The English International College, Spain

From Ending To Beginning

O how that too, too sullied flesh would melt,
Thaw and resolve itself into a dew;
Disapparition in my case would be felt,
As a pleasure, yet appetising to few.

Thaw and resolve itself into a dew;
To float between all matter and life,
As a pleasure, yet appetising to few.
I'd slaughter God Himself to end this strife.

To float between all matter and life
And mourn in a choir of demons.
I'd slaughter God Himself to end this strife,
Regardless of honesty, trust or my reasons.

And mourn in a choir of demons,
A song of tranquil revenge,
Regardless of honesty, trust or my reasons;
Greater evil lay here to avenge.

A song of tranquil revenge;
It deafens the most innocent ear.
Greater evil lay here to avenge,
Each particle of salt from each tiny tear.

It deafens the most innocent ear,
To hear of my unjustified fate,
Each particle of salt from each tiny tear;
The newborn babies with a newborn hate.

To hear of my unjustified fate,
Would do you no harm if you had felt,
The newborn babies with a newborn hate,
O how that too, too sullied flesh would melt.

Louise Edwards (16)
The English International College, Spain

Big City Life

Hard day at work,
Hard night at home,
Single mother working
Every day alone.

Working in a diner
To pay for my gin,
Sometimes I think
Where did it begin?

The bills are coming,
My head is sore,
Wish I could work
For a little bit more.

Picking up washing,
Mopping the floor,
Rent man is calling,
Knock, knock on my door.

Kids always screaming,
Head simply ringing,
Stab me with a knife,
End of city life.

Sean McConville (13)
The English International College, Spain

Stop And Stare

Forget what happened that day,
Forget what a treacherous time it was,
Forget what we saw
From the school front door.

Forget what happened when watching
The news with an open jaw,
Forget that scene that shocked the world,
Forget the shattered lives,
Forget the screams which weakened everyone's heart.

Remember the courageous people who care so much.

Alex Baines (12)
The English International College, Spain

Me And My School!

I'm on my way to school this morning,
Please, please don't let it be boring!

Maths, PE and English too,
These are the subjects I like to do!

But best of all are drama and art,
Because everybody can take part!

We go out to play with all the balls
And back in again when the lunch bell calls!

The afternoons can be really fun,
As we sometimes go on a long beach run!

It's where I go to meet my friends,
The time soon passes and another day ends!

Samantha Scott (12)
The English International College, Spain

Stay Safe

Stay in when there are fights
To delay your demise,
Stay in when it is night
If you don't want to die.

If you want to stay here,
Stay away from knives,
Stay away from guns
If you want to survive.

Stay away from the gangsters,
Stay in at night,
Stay in at day,
Stay in all your life.

Morgan Tudball (12)
The English International College, Spain

I Do Not Know

There's a girl on the windowpane,
She looks very dull,
But her skin as white as snow,
So it seems I do not know.

Is she an heiress
Or a beggar girl?
Did she come from Miss Minchin's?
I really do not know.

Why won't she speak?
She may be deaf,
She's like my friend Beth
And her name, I do not know.

Her name's Emingarud,
She was an heiress
Until her pa died,
Something made her cry, I do not know why.

Now she is a parlour maid,
Waits on hand and foot,
Secret visits from old friends,
Do they get caught? I do not know!

Cook shouts at her,
Scares her to death,
That's why she hardly ever speaks,
I think, does she ever weep? I do not know.

So now you know about this girl,
I do ask a lot of questions,
Will I ever meet you?
I do not know.

Lily Mae Silver (11)
The English International College, Spain

Demon Lover

(Inspired by 'Every You, Every Me' by Placebo)

I crave your feeling, don't dehumanise my heart;
What I want, what I need, I'd sacrifice my belief,
Your heart is a tart, and it plucks us so apart;
I gave you everything I had, your heart don't perceive.

What I want, what I need, I'd sacrifice my belief;
I beg you don't leave me behind, I lie here charmed,
I gave you everything I had, your heart don't perceive;
Another love I would abuse, now I am the one harmed.

I beg you don't leave me behind, I lie here charmed;
Will you love me any less, if I hurt you any more?
Another love I would abuse, now I am the one harmed;
I know I'm selfish, unkind, but you should ignore.

Will you love me any less, if I hurt you any more?
Your heart is a tart and it plucks us so apart,
I know I'm selfish, unkind, but you should ignore;
I crave your feeling, don't dehumanise my heart.

Bianca Wimmer
The English International College, Spain

To The Romantics

I believe I am no writer
And on thin water I do tread
When I, to find something to fight for,
Take the crown off the sovereign's head.
And despite the unkind remarks
I do persist to shout and yell
When in the discussion of Karl Marx
I condemn the capital to Hell.
I don't ever hide my visions,
Therefore they are invisible,
For to all those making decisions
One's life consists of just physicals.

They see no flying elephants
(Nor do the second see the first).
They live in count of their own triumphs
While all the time awaiting the worst,
And while indiscreetly laughing
And while tapping their goddamn feet,
I am through the endless air soaring
Next to the sails of the mind's mighty fleet.

The king's invisible clothes I saw
The day my brown shuttered eyes saw fit.
'Twas then I became a thief
To take ink from my book's pages
And in my far land as a Sikh
I spit at the politics' rages.
And thus I, by blithe's mind will ask
'Share Skylark! All you have with me,'
And no burden weighed on this task,
I'll sit on the branches of wisdom's tree.

Elene Kotetishvili (16)
The English International College, Spain

Age Of Four

I remember, I remember age four
High enough to see the kitchen tables
Also high enough to open the door
I'm afraid I still sucked the kitchen ladles.

I remember, I remember age four
I loved to listen to jokes ha, ha
Using my imagination I saw
White sheep prancing around singing baa, baa.

I remember, I remember age four
I was just about to start my new school
I was always playing with my toy boar
I also found a way to sit on a stool.

I remember, I remember age four
I will be age four, no more, no more.

Douglas Cameron-Hobbs (11)
The English International College, Spain

The Haunted Poem

There is something different about this house,
In every corner a creep of a mouse.
The walls are slimy and falling apart,
You think this is bad, this is only the start,
I hear strange noises from the doors,
I hear howling within the floors.
People speak while I'm asleep,
They creep and weep and creep and weep.
I see people walking the halls,
I hear them scream their horrible calls.
Why do you think this is a place I would stay?
By now you'd think I'd run away,
So this is all I have to say,
Too bad for me this is where I stay.

Georgina Sinclair (12)
The English International College, Spain

Alone

I walk these empty streets
And glance towards the deserted tree
With nothing to lead but my feet.
I listen for the humming of the bee
Hell must have no company.

I, a spider caught in this web
Searching a way to set myself free
But how I dread
How do I bring myself glee?
How do I flee?

I'm looking for an easy way out
But still I wonder
I want to go without a shout
But for that I ponder
The decision comes like thunder.

I peer over the ledge
Look down below
Jump off the edge
Into the turbulent flow
I have nowhere else to go.

Conor McCarthy (13)
The English International College, Spain

Surreal

You cannot hear me,
You think I'm not real
Everything is eerie
Everything must be surreal

You think I'm not real
Just 'cause you don't believe
Everything must be surreal
I just wish I could leave

Just 'cause you don't believe
You judge me and tease me
I just wish I could leave
There's nothing left to please me

You judge me and tease me
Everything is eerie
There's nothing left to please me
You cannot hear me

Daniella Franken (12)
The English International College, Spain

Thirteen

Thirteen
Awkward age
Hormones are keen
Running with rage

Awkward age
I've got loads of spots
Running with rage
I've got the grots

I've got loads of spots
They are driving me mad
I've got the grots
When I reach twenty-one I'll sure be glad

They are driving me mad
Hormones are keen
When I reach twenty-one I'll sure be glad
Thirteen.

Josh Taggart (13)
The English International College, Spain

Lies

All along it was all just lies
You must have thought that I was blind
I don't think you realise how I've cried
You were wrong if you thought I wouldn't mind

You must have thought that I was blind
It's as if my world just went black
You were wrong if you thought I wouldn't mind
I just wish things would go back

It's as if my world just went black
I don't want things to end
I just wish things would go back
My broken heart will never mend

I don't want things to end
I don't think you realise how much I've cried
My broken heart will never mend
All along it was all just lies.

Candice Fox (14)
The English International College, Spain

Being A Teenager Sucks

I just wish I was five again,
Nothing to worry about.
And there is no pain,
When you could just shout.

Nothing to worry about,
Everything closes in.
When you could just shout,
I've been placed in the bin.

Everything closes in,
I'm like a very bad trend.
I've been placed in the bin,
And it drives me around the bend.

I just wish I was five again,
My mum doesn't even tuck me in.
And there is no pain,
But it doesn't matter, put me in a tin.

Denny South (13)
The English International College, Spain

Don't Look, Don't Stare, Get Away From Me!

Don't ever look at me
Don't even dare.
Just don't, I don't want you to see.
Not a glimpse, not even a quick stare.

Don't even dare!
Please don't look, it's just intolerable.
Not a glimpse, not even a quick stare!
Don't look, don't stare, I'm just so horrible.

Please don't it's just intolerable
Why would you want to look? Why would you care?
Don't look, don't stare, I'm just so horrible.
I know you will even laugh at the clothes I wear.

Why would you want to look? Why would you care?
Just don't, I don't want you to see.
I know you will even laugh at the clothes I wear.
Don't ever look at me!

Lucas Whittaker (13)
The English International College, Spain

The Virgin Vixen

The virgin vixen lives in hiding
on the priory land of lemon groves and strawberry fields,
she nourishes on citrus fruits,
of all kinds,
yet desires her animal instinct.

Her exceptional complexion makes others crave her attractiveness,
she's an addict to herself.

She absorbs her loneliness within her beauty
and seeks to find true love.

She spends many days prowling around her forbidden lands,
which have not yet been stepped onto
dreaming of her
fantasy fox,
to unite as one.

To unlock the secret that is her virginity
and swear her undying love.

Melanie Fievet & Abie Taggart (15)
The English International College, Spain

No One Knows What It's Like To Be Me

No one knows what it's like to be me
Having to be someone I'm not
All I want to be is the real me
But yet I'm still not

Having to be someone I'm not
I feel like I'm being compressed
But I'm still not the real me
So when people see me I look depressed

I feel like I'm being compressed
I want my spirit to be free
So when people see me I look depressed
Will no one ever let me be?

I want my spirit to be free
Sometimes I feel like it's the end
Will no one ever let me be
But then I feel I'm on the mend.

Zareena Fitchett (14)
The English International College, Spain

I Love My Lips

If my lips ever left my mouth,
Packed a bag and headed south.
That'd be too bad,
I'd be so sad.

If my lips said adios,
I don't like you, I think you're gross.
That's be too bad,
I'd call my dad.

If my lips moved to the loose,
Left a dime and took my tooth.
That'd be too bad,
I might get mad.

When I was just two years old,
I left my lips out in the cold
And they turned blue,
What could I do?

Ten days after I turned eight,
Got my lips stuck in a gate
So I'm saying,
I love my lips!

William Wheeler (11)
The English International College, Spain

In The Morning

Early in the morn,
People are fast asleep,
Not making a sound,
Cock-a-doodle-doo
A cockerel cries,
Alarm clocks go off too,
People yawn as they get up,
The light shines through the curtains,
Their eyes, nearly blinded by the sun,
Time for breakfast,
All get dressed
And off to school we go.

Nadine Calmfors (12)
The English International College, Spain

Found Poem

The wind, frantically powerful around his head,
His body, sculptured around the rocks,
Inside the house, the dog whimpered,
Sunlight, scrubbing his face with light,
Grass whistled around his disarming face,
Umbrellas lashed around in the wind,
Young faces complacently quiet,
In the trees, the birds whistled, twisted and turned,
Some leaves, scrubbing his face,
Disarmingly quiet, nature all around,
Earned his own sculptured place on the hill,
As he quietly lay, disarmingly,
Down the twisted hill.

Matthew Doe (14)
The English International College, Spain

Time Awakened

The dark, angry clouds flocked together,
Pellucid flashes of lightning struck the land and thrashed the air.
On top of a fluffy, green-grassed hill sat a girl,
Hair like yellow hay, brittle and thin.
Her stare was sharpening and figuring.
She sat over a deep green pool
With a powerful yet motionless appearance to her face.
Wind moved among the leaves
And whistled through the soft, fluffy grass.
Her face was ageless,
After staring at the green pool
She lifted her head up.
Time awakened.

Aimee Watkinson (15)
The English International College, Spain

Sun Down, Down In The Old Town

I looked into a half opened door
The cone of the shade threw its brightness straight downward;
It was late in the afternoon
The kids came to play at our place.
There were old men sitting on old and crunchy chairs
With shapeless hats on their old grey heads.
Young labouring men with sleepy faces
Were going to work after a siesta.
Sun down was approaching:
The blue sky of an autumn day
The red light dimmed on the coals
'Come boy, come on'
You could hear parents shout out the window
While their children were playing football.
I saw boys trying to disengage their ears from their parents' hands
Because they would not go inside to have dinner.
Five minutes later
A silence fell
From the dark sky
Of the old town
Marbella.

Ricardo Bocanegra Yebra (15)
The English International College, Spain

All This Terror Unleashed On The World

I'm watching the news and I'm sad
I can't believe what I'm seeing.
What's happening out there is bad
Anger and fear is what I'm feeling.

I can't believe what I'm seeing
What's going on in the world?
Anger and fear's what I'm feeling
All this terror that has been unfurled.

What's going on in the world?
I'm seeing what damage is done
All this terror that has been unfurled
Want the victims to see the sun.

I'm seeing what damage is done
What's happening out there is bad
Want the victims to see the sun
I'm watching the news and I'm sad.

Josie Craigs (16)
The English International College, Spain

That One Thing That Makes You Feel

The way music makes me feel
Ever heard of grunge?
Kurt Cobain, Frank Lero, it's just so real
The feeling of darkness makes me plunge.

Ever heard of grunge?
I love it more than anything
The feeling of darkness makes me plunge
It's the way they play and sing.

I love it more than anything
It can make me laugh, smile and cry
It's the way they play and sing
If you don't like it, you'll love it once you try

It can make me laugh, smile and cry
Kurt Cobain, Frank Lero, it's just so real
If you don't like it, you'll love it once you try
The way music makes me feel.

Maneli Golbacheh (14)
The English International College, Spain

The Call Of A Deathbed

I wander alone,
Street by street.
In a world unknown,
Given up to defeat.

My eyes begin to sting,
From tears that come from my soul.
My ears can't hear, my mouth can't sing,
My heart as burnt as coal.

The rain falls down on my face,
The tears of a mourning god.
My heart increases its pace,
My body caught in a rod.

I look around at other people,
Can feel their warmth calling.
I feel like I'm on a steeple,
For my life is just as appalling.

It's not all just a nightmare,
A horse appearing in flight.
This is true, a warning glare,
For I may not be here tonight.

Bruno Micchiardi (13)
The English International College, Spain

Between Love And Hate

Between love and hate
In a world where love has run out
The angel just says wait
And hate is all about.

In a world where love has run out
Where the sky is closing in
And hate is all about
It's like committing a sin.

Where the sky is closing in
I need to break free
It's like committing a sin
Happiness is the key.

I need to break free
The angel just says wait
Happiness is the key
Between love and hate.

Charlotte Alexander (14)
The English International College, Spain

The Meeting

He advanced a step onto the path
Tense and motionless.
She looked at him, smiled archly and twitched her body.
A far rush of wind drove through her hair,
As the shade climbed up the hill.
She spoke with a friendly tone.
'I get lonely, I have no one to talk to.'
He invited confidence without demanding it.
'I would do better without you.'
She ached for attention
As he backed towards the trees again.
The forest was darkening.

Natasha Franken (14)
The English International College, Spain

Observe

The deep green pool,
Twisted and turned,
Her hair hung in little rolled clusters,
His hands, large and lean,
She smiled complacently,
His huge companion dropped his blankets and sat,
A moment settled, hovered and moved on.
He invited confidence without demanding it,
Her disarming smile defeated him.
The shadow in the valley became blue
And the evening came fast.

Charlee Eason (14)
The English International College, Spain

A Lonely Girl

Motionless and waiting, stood a girl looking in,
Her face was sweet and young
And her lips were parched,
She had a nasal, brittle quality
And was very pretty and simple.
Suddenly the halter chains clinked
And the men's voices became louder,
A far rush of wind sounded
And there she lay,
Motionless, half covered in hay.

Tom Foster (14)
The English International College, Spain

Heaven

She smiled beautifully
Like a lover's voice on a late morning,
He whispered and chuckled softly at his own joke.
Dark of face, with restless eyes
His disarming smile defeated her
She could not move.
She wanted to kiss him lightly on the cheek.
All this made her crazy,
They were trapped in this perfect world.
Tense and motionless
She could not play pretend,
This little girl's grown up by now
Almost.
Not quite.
The whole damn world is scared of each other.
And as our Heavens expanded,
The end came away
These were my dreams on Earth.

Jordana Dias (14)
The English International College, Spain

I Remember, I Remember

I remember, I remember
When my best friend ran away.
Her dad waited at the airport
She told me not to say.

I remember, I remember
When her mum realised she had gone.
The panic on her face, as she called her on the phone.
My best friend didn't answer, as her dad John said, 'No!'

I remember, I remember
As her family fought and fought;
Uncles, aunties, grandparents, Mum and Dad
And she stood there, in deep thought.

I remember, I remember
When her dad won the fight.
On the plane back to Ireland
She slept happily through the night.

Danielle Kinnen
The English International College, Spain

Thinking About A Boy

Breaking, healing, thinking about a boy,
I miss your scent, your kiss, your smile, your touch,
My soul tarnished, broken, half dead, destroyed,
I wish it was real, I wish it so much.

I miss your scent, your kiss, your smile, your touch,
Can feel your fingerprints still on my heart,
I wish it was real, I wish it so much,
I love you still, it's ripping me apart.

Can feel your fingerprints still on my heart,
Hating that your kiss is no longer mine,
I love you still, it's ripping me apart,
I would move the Earth to turn back the time.

Hating that your kiss is no longer mine,
Your love got me so high, I was floating,
I would move the Earth to turn back the time,
But it was poison in candy coating.

Your love got me so high, I was floating,
My hearts may fall, but won't change anything,
But it was poison in candy coating,
Trying to fly with ripped, broken wings.

My tears may fall, but won't change anything,
Now I know the truth, now I feel the pain,
But it was poison in candy coating,
The world seems pointless, worthless, dead, mundane.

Now I know the truth, now I feel the pain,
My soul tarnished, broken, half dead, destroyed,
The world seems pointless, worthless, dead, mundane,
Breaking, healing, thinking about a boy.

Sasha Lauren Campbell (16)
The English International College, Spain

Mist

The mist circles in
Clouds up the mind
Lost from all but kin
But you're one of my kind

Clouds up in the mind
When I see you a veil is lifted
But you're one of my kind
My dreams with you are twisted

When I see you a veil is lifted
I wanna be with you
My dreams with you are twisted
I wish this were not true

I wanna be with you
Lost from all but kin
I wish this were not true
The mist circles in.

Benjamin Matthews (14)
The English International College, Spain

The Crimson Angel

The crimson angel
Inhabits the untouched parts of the world,
In secret lands, too beautiful for the eyes of man
Amongst the never-ending blossom orchards
And the rolling dunes of honeycomb beaches.

The angels do not feel the need to eat
They are beyond this desire
Because they are simply the creation of a perfect harmony
They sustain their lives on all that is pure
They could not survive in our tainted world
For man is the only thing that could destroy these mythical creatures.

The angels are born with a soulmate
With love for each other in their souls
They stay together for the centuries that are their lives
They show no signs of age, but when the time comes
And their destiny is fulfilled they come together one last time to die
They burn out bright in a brilliant supernova of love
And this is how a new crimson angel is born.

Tom King (16)
The English International College, Spain

The Angel

Now I'm lying on the pavement,
I can't fight back the tear.
The pain is too much to handle,
The sound of sirens is all I hear.

The angel came down to me
And told me not to cry.
She asked if I would go with her
And then she whispered why.

I dried my eyes and sat straight up
And she reached out for my hand.
Suddenly I wasn't hurting
As she took me to her distant land.

Heaven was its name I think
With lots of white and gold.
Although now I wish I hadn't come
Before my time, before I'm old.

Clara King (14)
The English International College, Spain